# Mud in Magic

by

Beverly M. Collins

**Books of Poetry by Moonrise Press**

Maja Trochimczyk, *Miriam's Iris or Angels in the Garden* (2008)
Maja Trochimczyk, *Rose Always – A Court Love Story* (2008, rev. 2011)
Ed Rosenthal, *The Desert Hat* (2013)
Marlene Hitt, *Clocks and Water Drops* (2015)
Beverly M. Collins, *Mud in Magic* (2015)

**Poetry Anthologies**

Maja Trochimczyk, ed., *Chopin with Cherries: A Tribute in Verse* (2010)
Maja Trochimczyk, ed., *Meditations on Divine Names* (2012)

# Mud in Magic

Poems by

Beverly M. Collins

Los Angeles, 2015

*Mud in Magic* by Beverly M. Collins

**This book is published by Moonrise Press**
P.O. Box 4288, Los Angeles – Sunland
CA 91041-4288, www.moonrisepress.com
info@moonrisepress.com

© Copyright 2015 by Beverly M. Collins and Moonrise Press.
The prior publication of the following poems is hereby gratefully acknowledged:
- "In Whispers," *The Altadena Poetry Review 2015 Anthology*, Golden Foothill Press (Spring 2015)
- "Petal Gossip," *San Gabriel Valley Poetry Quarterly* 61 (Winter 2014)
- "Beyond Me," *San Gabriel Valley Poetry Quarterly* issue 65 (Winter 2015)
- "Son of Cement," *PoeticDiversity.org* (November 2014)
- "Down South Summer," *San Gabriel Valley Poetry Quarterly* 62 (Spring 2014)
- "Dear Picasso," *San Gabriel Valley Poetry 2014 Calendar* (January 2014)
- "Bona Fide Valentine," *Fiesta of Love Anthology,* (Spring 2013), Writer's Empire and *Free Love 2* Anthology (February 2014)
- "Broom Repair," *Nightmares* Anthology (November 2013)
- "Twin Light," *Poetry Super Highway* (Summer 2013)
- "All In A Day," *San Gabriel Valley Poetry Quarterly* 59 (Summer 2013)
- Uncle John Ames," *California Quarterly,* Vol. 38, No. 3 & 4 (2012)
- "Morning Moonrise," "Balloon Life," "The Loudest Voice," *Patch.com*(2011)
- "Alabama Hills," *Painted My Way*, Poets on Site (September 2011)
- "The Mist," *Poetry Letter and Literary Review*, CSPS (December 2010)

© Copyright 2015 by Beverly M. Collins, Cover Photographs (sun in clouds, and mud), Used by Permission in a Cover Design by Maja Trochimczyk

All Rights Reserved 2015 by Moonrise Press
*No part of this book may be reproduced or utilized in any form or by any means, electronic or mechanical, including photocopying and recording, or by any information storage and retrieval system, without permission in writing from the publisher. This book is simultaneously published in print and e-book editions.*

**Manufactured in the United States of America**

**The Library of Congress Publication Data:**
Collins, Beverly M., 1958–
[Poems. English]
Mud in Magic/ Beverly M. Collins, author
118 pages (xviii pp. + 78 pp.) 15.2 cm x 22.9 cm. Written in English.
    Includes 65 poems, acknowledgments and a portrait.
    ISBN 978-0-9963981-0-7 (paperback)
    ISBN 978-0-9963981-1-4 (e-book, E-Pub format)
    I. Collins, Beverly M., 1958 – Poetry. II. Title.

10 9 8 7 6 5 4 3 2 1

# PREFACE

I am pleased to present to the readers the fourth volume in our series dedicated to the talents and achievements of female poets. I first met Beverly as a poet writing stories and poems for children. These genres are still very important in her oeuvre and the present volume includes a fair share of humorous verse destined primarily for children. But it is more than that. Beverly M. Collins's *Mud in Magic* is her second poetry book. Her previous volume, *Quiet Observations*, gathered reflections about the quirky, delightful, charming and surprising aspects of life, seen, as it were, through the rosy glasses of compassion and good humor. *Mud in Magic* is the next stage in this journey. There's wisdom of experience in her poetry, wisdom that has grown from a life well lived.

Her poetry is very much like the poet – kind, witty, and observant, filled with insights into the human experience and the passage of time. Aconsummate ethics teacher at heart, she fashions from images and similes life-skills lessons for herself and for others. Yet, Beverly does not appear to treat herselfnor the world too seriously: she is well aware of the healing force of laughter, and the continuous presence of bits of "mud in magic."

In these poems, styled as messages and postcards from the Thought Bistro (Part I) and Elixir Café (Part III), there is no intent to shock just tospuriously shock or horrify the readers. Her words contain no hate, no purposeful aggravation. The poems are filled with light and love – the latter, in its many reincarnations, from the affectionate to wistful, to, again, humorous – is the subject of the central part of the book, Tinder Flames.

In vain you would search here for empty fireworks of verbal displays. Beverly's skillful and often aphoristic or narrative poems portray a scene or a character that we could encounter on our streets, in our cafes. The beauty and wonder of daily life fills the pages and, we hope, will delight our readers.

*Dr. Maja Trochimczyk, Publisher*

# Acknowledgments

Almighty Spirit that lovingly supports and beckons us all in being our best selves. The warm memory of my parents, Raymond and Roberta Moses. To Michelle L. Collins, Miles J. Mallier and Carol T. Mallier for your listening ear on my new pieces. Hugs to my sisters, Deborah E. Collins, Sheila M. Johnson and lots of love to my entire family and thriving circle of dear friends.

A big thank you to Maja Trochimczyk, Moonrise Press and to the editors and publishers that have previously included my poems in their publications, some of which appear in this book and to those who continuously support my work: Don Kingfisher Campbell, Thelma T. Reyna, Marie Lecrivain, James Levin, Dorothy Skiles, Marlene Hitt, Kath Abela Wilson, Jessica Wilson Cardenas, Radomir Vojtech Luza, Mary Anneeta Mann, Russell Salamon, Joe DeCenzo, Jessica Ceballos, Apryl Skies, D.M. Collins, Rick Lupert, D. Marlar, Lady Lazarus Press, Writer's Empire, Sybaritic Press, Sourcebooks Inc., The Educator-National NFED Newsletter and Ragan Communications Inc.

The author gratefully acknowledges the following publishers for previously including earlier versions of her poems in their anthologies and periodicals.

- "In Whispers" in *The Altadena Poetry Review 2015 Anthology*, Golden Foothill Press (Spring 2015)
- "Beyond Me" in *San Gabriel Valley Poetry Quarterly* issue 65 (Winter 2015)
- "Son of Cement," *PoeticDiversity.org* (November 2014)
- "Petal Gossip" in *San Gabriel Valley Poetry Quarterly* issue 61 (Winter 2014)
- "Down South Summer" in *San Gabriel Valley Poetry Quarterly* issue 62 (Spring 2014)
- "Dear Picasso" in *San Gabriel Valley Poetry 2014 Calendar* (January 2014)

- "Bona Fide Valentine" in *Fiesta of Love Anthology,* (Spring 2013), Writer's Empire and *Free Love 2* Anthology (February 2014)
- "Broom Repair" in *Nightmares* Anthology (November 2013)
- "All In A Day" in *San Gabriel Valley Poetry Quarterly* issue 59 (Summer 2013)
- "Uncle John Ames" in *California Quarterly,* Vol. 38, No. 3 & 4 (California State Poetry Society,) 2012
- Morning Moonrise," "Balloon Life" and "The Loudest Voice" on *Patch.com* (Spring 2011)
- "Twin Light" in *Poetry Super Highway* (Summer 2013)
- "Alabama Hills" in *Painted My Way*, Poets on Site (September 2011)
- "The Mist" in *Poetry Letter and Literary Review*, CSPS (December 2010)

*~Beverly M. Collins*

# Contents

**I. Thought Bistro—•—1**

Stew —•—2
Forward—•—3
Hammer—•—5
Down South Summer—•—6
Cake—•—7
Balloon Life—•—8
Petal Gossip—•—10
Flowers—•—11
Autumn—•—12
Broom Repair—•—13
Chisel—•—14
Bone Marrow Carol—•—15
Stay—•—16
The Arrangement—•—17
Ten Lessons from Raymond—•—18
Uncle John Ames—•—19
Son of Cement—•—20
Beyond Me—•—21
The Loudest Voice—•—22
Bursting at the Seems—•—23
For Goodness Sake—•—24
Beautiful—•—25
Dear Picasso—•—26
Misfire—•—27
Lost and Round—•—28
Can You Believe?—•—29

## II. Tinder Flames—•—31

In Whispers—•—32
Twin Light—•—33
The Stone—•—34
Soul Season—•—35
Bona Fide Valentine—•—36
Damsel—•—37
Loitering in the Doorway—•—38
The Offering —•—39
Paperweight—•—40
Prey—•—41
Quake—•—42
Un-Intimacy—•—43
Bat of the Eye—•—44
Still Life with Bird—•—45
Betrothal to Etch—•—46
Desire—•—47
Couple —•—48

## III. Elixir Cafe—•—49

Mud in Magic—•—50
Alabama Hills—•—51
Up for Air—•—52
Stitches—•—53
Until Now—•—54
Compassion—•—55
Saturday—•—56
Morning Moonrise—•—57
All in a Day—•—58
Later —•—59
Next—•—61
Made in...—•—62
Traveler—•—63
Walls Fell Down – Arrival in India—•—64

The Mist—•—65
Spiral—•—66
A Tune—•—67
Smitten—•—68
God Is—•—69
Home Sweet Home—•—70
Chapter Done—•—71
The Back Word—•—72

**About the Poet —•—75**

Dedication:

In loving celebration of all
who presently inspire
the world of Art.
I thank you!

# Mud in Magic

Beverly M. Collins

# I.

# Thought Bistro

**Stew**

It takes all kinds to fill the world
Dash of grit here, over there...
A colorful pinch of flower.
A room of twinkling eyes
Review a bewitching hour.

All for one – oh, really?
Is that how the saying goes?
Plant that sign in the center
Like the tip of a nose.

The old reach down.
The young reach up.
Some spin in the middle,
Reach for – they don't know what.

On the horizon,
A new day powders its face,
Waves fond farewell
To the night it replaced.

This thoughtful batch of words
Become tangy word-stew
To stir, poke and ponder.
Which parts are untrue?

# Forward

Forward can show up with a
hat on backwards in disguise.
Forward can spring from still
Places, we first don't recognize.

Forward loves Focus, can take
the appearance of a Step Back.
Hungers for the taste of perfect
order as we draw what we attract.

Rush can be a revolving door
that lands us where we started.
Demand can lead us to the room
Satisfaction just departed.

Anxious may not appeal to Forward
as it darts and jumps about.
Sly can lose sight of Forward.
Weaves webs, but won't move out.

Those who try to bully Forward,
often lose Balance. Seduction
may not move Forward while it tries
to take the place of Talent.

Jealousy can be found stuck in ditches
along the road with Grudge, too weighted down
to move its heavy load.

Honesty holds a bright light that shines
to Wisdom station. Humility points the way,
moves hand-in-hand with Patience.

Tolerance holds a master plan and turns
away from the Ego's muddle.
Understanding with Compassion brings
us Forward without Struggle.

# Hammer

If I had a hammer, I would hang this picture
purchased at the art show three weeks ago.
As I lift the picture from its temporary spot-in-corner,
I become a question mark with a pulse.

Do I have the proper nails to do the job?
Is this the right spot for the picture?
Is this spot too high?
Is it too low?
Is it slightly crooked?
Does the picture frame match the room?
Do I like the color of the wall?

If I had a hammer, with the right nails,
some good measuring tape and a proper
color paint, I would hang this picture.

But for now (just for now) I lean the picture
back in its temporary spot and notice
the face is sadder. Eyes question
like a child banished to the corner
for yet another time out.

## Down-South Summer

There was an extended sisterhood in the
warm circle of my "country-cousins."

Summer heat had a zip code
on curvy black paved roads
with ditches that eavesdropped
on our giggly-girl-talk.

Hopeful over our latest crushes,
we were half-bold, half-shy,
boy-crazy, empty-headed and
full of belief that we knew it all.

Thrilled to wear clothes too revealing
for our years that drew attention
we couldn't handle.

Baby deer caught in the headlights
of awkward adolescence. The black-hole
of our existence was being left out or left behind.

We watered dreams of a Grand Future.
All it needed was Me-plus-Time
then-Stir. We made long "to-do" lists.
I still attempt to check-off mine today.

Send in the Clowns!

# Cake

Blind of ingredients
before it was baked,

we stare at icing.
Does the menu say...cake?

From across the room,
the mouth starts to water.

We dash to the counter.
Oh, how quickly we order.

Fluffy and moist
it appears to the eye.

Sugary scent in the air
furthers the lie.

The unknowing and hungry
can hardly wait.

They take in big mouthfuls
Of unsweetened cake.

## Balloon Life

So there I loomed. Bloated and stretched to the limit.
A floating wall flower bouncing slightly
over a round wooden table  supporting a fluffy cake
of white butter cream frosting, with blue and red writing.

I noticed  the words – Happy, Birthday –
written on both myself and Fluffy Cake.
I thought to myself: Are we related?

I was about to ask when several gleeful humans
of different heights, shapes and genders
 entered the area. They glanced at us
with a smile and continued to talk amongst themselves.

Fluffy Cake  and I remained silent.

I wondered what Fluffy Cake was thinking
as one human pushed waxy sticks
into the icing and lit the ends with fire.

What?! I felt a pang of guilt as I did nothing
to come to Fluffy Cake's defense. The humans
very loudly sang a song
in unison. The same words! Written on myself
and Fluffy Cake!

The song ended and they blew out the fires
they had lit only moments earlier.
They clapped their hands and cheered.
What a strange ritual. Strange – these humans.

All at once, a knife was drawn and I witnessed
the assassination of Fluffy Cake.

I did not want to look
but had no way of turning away.
The humans then used prong-like instruments
to scoop Fluffy Cake into their
mouths!

Oh, the Horror!

Moments later, a young female human
reached toward me with an open safety pin.
Who's safety? Certainly not mine,
for with one deadly caress -

POW!

I was a goner!

## Petal Gossip

Pollen is all the rage
as buds awaken and  wings flutter.

There have been shocking
reports of a band of snails
sneaking like pirates and

unruly Dandelions screaming
that they are yellow too,
openly at the Sun.

Our sources tell us:
Red is the new Red,
Pink has paled in comparison
and some leaves have curled
Green with envy.

This is Lana-Lady-Bug here,
reporting live from the edge
of the flower-bed.
Stay tuned for more
of "Life Among Roses."

## Flowers

A welcome sight for sore eyes:
one signal of a season. Token of
love, or grief, or just because,
sometimes the only reason.

The flower's cycle mirrors ours
from bud to rose to petals fallen.
We brave wind and rain just like
flowers as new awakenings
come-a-calling.

Let your colors burst on display.
Bloom new buds with each new day.
Like a subtle base of fine perfume,
be the centerpiece that brightens a room.

## Autumn

Autumn blows away the heat of Summer
dazzles with a dance of deep-burned colors,

The year exfoliates itself – we watch in wonder.

On cool winds, whispered promises
of sure fun. Witches, turkeys and Santa
all soon to come.

Marching on the heels of Autumn.

From our upstairs window, we can see
a seasonal show, until Autumn hides again
under a blanket of snow.

When Autumn dips away, we feel no concern.
On a merry-go-round of seasons it will
always return.

With a big colorful Autumn smile on its face.

## Broom Repair

A toothless, gaunt and warted witch
stopped in for some repairs. "Hello" – she called
into the Auto shop. At first, saw no one there.

From under a car, a mechanic rolled out
and asked, "Can I help you?"

"Sonny, I hope you can." She croaked –
as the man looked up and stared.

"I'm-a-needing help with my old ride,
do you give broom repair?"

"Broom Repair! Why that's silly" – he snapped,
Is this some kind of a joke?"

Sadly, that was the very last words
he ever spoke. She turned the mechanic

into a frog with one swish
of her stubby wand. Then she calmly
sat on her back-firing broom
and she was gone.

# Chisel

As I wash my face one evening in my bathroom,
Ponder rises from the steam curled with the heat.

I am suddenly aware that in 200 years
my nose could disappear from all my pictures
like some of the statues of Egypt.
Even small statues were not safe.

Historians may say it was caused by
a thousand miniature chisels in the wind
that leave the shape of the ear untouched:
This "breaking-wind" only wants the nose.

Yo-ho, little tiny wind-pirates!
They probably have caves of stolen noses
hidden somewhere in the hills.
Only bats view them.

This is the fly-paper story some historians
are stuck to. It can be found flourishing,
wherever bridges are sold.

## Bone Marrow Carol

Hear the echo of all the New Jersey towns
from childhood. I called them home.
My love for Dominick ringing still
in the center, of the **very** center,
of the center of my bones.

Grand moments and false starts huddle,
shoulder to shoulder, like sheep.
Unfed dreams tightly swaddled,
humming still fast asleep.

My little girl giggles and hiccups.
My teenage self throws tantrums and cries.
All the love I sent out and took in
through my eyes.

Deep-toned inspirational words
from the Apostles
and a few memories welcomed
as morning breath to a nostril.

Life impact chimes clearly.
As clear as can get.
Each new day adds new notes.
It is not over yet.

## Stay

"Stay as you are." The gentleman waved,
as he tipped his hat.

"What a pipe-dream," I mumbled, there
is no chance of that.

Stay as I am?

Was he so fooled by a smile?
Switched on charm with canned
laughter pulled from a file.

Stay What?

Single, with a head-cold, waiting for the bus?

Stay...
In a crappy apartment, with room-mates
I don't trust?

Stay...
Invisible to the people that I most respect?

Stay...
Snippy, with an attitude I need to correct?

Stay...
Determined to go further than my parents went,
with all these books in my lap?

Oh! What?

Maybe, that's what he meant.

## The Arrangement

They say he was taught in stern, layered lessons
from his favorite chair  as a child. This was once
his Grand-Daddy's shop. Then, his Daddy's shop.

Yet, he was friendly as black mold with a steely
disposition you could break your teeth on. Requests
over his counter were met with slow movements
and the charm of a prodded crocodile.

Why had he traded the breath of enthusiasm
for the thorny underside of his "safe choice?"
The same rat corner, same shop,
this quicksand year into the next.

Was he silent-auctioned into entrapment?
A vine that chokes with time creeping slow.
Strong scent all it's own, broken flowers to show.
His dreams drown in the waters that were
their wishes? Burnt away with every cigar sold?

Evenings called him to an upstairs porch
where he lightly chewed dissatisfaction
on his lower lip and stared intently at everything
below and nothing in particular. What were
the unshared reasons he agreed to this arrangement?

# Ten Lessons from Raymond

## Taught by Example

Patience is a key.
Thoughtfulness can get you in the door.
Kindness can keep you in the room.
Empathy can place you permanently within a heart.
Listeners learn – so listen, listen, listen.
Composure is an asset that you can carry with you
at all times.
Being firm should stop short of being harsh.
Bigheartedness can show itself in the smallest of
gestures.
Snowball fights and hot soup should be a package deal.
Men get their hearts broken too.

Thanks for the stories. Even our debates were fun.
Thanks for our talks about everything under the sun.
You gave the title, **Stepfather** a good name
for stepfathers everywhere. You could have taught
my birth-father the many facets of how to care.

# Uncle John Ames

An old man came to slumber
kept company with crickets
and cracking wood.

"Well, how do ya do there?"
He called out to no-one
As cheerfully as he could.

The chipped paint stared loud
with silence, the stove hummed
low its same  song.

Cups and plates gave their attention
stacked neat and clean
where they belonged.
He blinked through cigar smoke,
he saw her!

Over a yellow bowl
she stirred her loving spoon.
The fleeting glimpse gave a signal
they would be back together soon.

## Son of Cement

He descends down the stairs of the tattered
tan building as if his feet are on a course
to his breech rebirth. A mere chip pounding
the pavement of an old block he grew from.

He projects an attitude as bold as
the thick-linked chain around his neck
for all to see. He feigns an ego so big
 the wave from it could help the fishermen,
on the edge of town, propel their boats.

His shoulders: a show of pride as he
swaggers forward in uneven stomp-steps,
his gaze darts quickly left, then right, then
left again, as if somewhere along this street,
in a blanket of half-light.

Somewhere, lounging on a café window-sill
or circling like a moth around a street lamp
or flung along the grit of the curb near the
corner, he could find that long lost piece
of himself.

# Beyond Me

I see the homeless
as I walk or drive by.
I look away fast should their
glance meet my eye.
The pain that they live in is beyond me.

I hear parts of the news
as I channel surf.
I mute it or tune out
for all its worth.
Those dramatic reports are beyond me.

My co-workers – laid off
But for now, I am spared
I swallow back hard
over time that we shared
Hope their loss of wage is beyond me.

Someone poisoned the water
I hope "they" clean it up.
The problem is way over there
I shrug sipping my cup.
A mistake – I think it's beyond me.

## The Loudest Voice

Provocative echo shook the land
called wolf and sheep to follow.

Slaughter house filler's quest to
feed a place within that's hollow.

All content is on display.
Not seeing is a choice.

Bandwagon jumpers went off
the cliff following the loudest voice.

## Bursting at the Seems

He leans forward lifts the corner of the blind at his front
window. Fragile secret spy on unofficial afternoon duty.
First report: it seems his neighbor Jeff shows evidence
that he had too much Saturday-evening-sauce on a Thursday
night. His car is parked crooked; the back sticks too far
out in the street, the front pushed right against the curb.

In other news, it seems like something has dug up
a part of Judy's flower bed again. It seems whatever keeps
digging up her flowers, likes marigolds. She should try
some other flower and rap the roots.

Oh, no! It seems Bob and Jessica have a cavalcade of company
pouring in again. "Seems we are in for another loud party
of pool splashing and scream/laughing"–he mumbles to
himself.

He notices a man with a clip board leaving his neighbors'
house. The man seems to be headed in his direction.
It's 1:40 in the afternoon. Not wanting to be solicited,
surveyed or caught playing hooky from life in dark-blue, torn
underwear, he lets go of the blind and steps back…
on an envelope lying of the floor. He looks down
and sees it is a part of a posse of envelopes called
Yesterday's Mail. They are hanging out on the floor,
hoping to get discovered someday.

He looks up, holds very still, listens for the man's footsteps
on the walk. He hears nothing, but sees a cobweb dancing
above him. It seems to just dare him to dust it. Just to its
right it has a neighbor; a fresh web… with a spider
in the middle. It lifts one strand, it peeks at him…
or so it seems.

# For Goodness Sake

*Step One*

A muted middle-aged couple stare at each other and blink slowly. Then, they quickly interrupt this pregnant pause with the roar of a drunken argument.

*Step Two*

They exhaust themselves back into sober silence when a hot-tempered guy seated nearby takes a stance and asks them to chill.

*Step Three*

This causes a long-legged lady who listens and leans in the lounge to literally laugh...
until she cries.

*A Four-Step Dance?*

No! Here they go again!

# Beautiful

Beautiful – wobbly first
steps of the toddler.
Sparkling new sprout on
the family tree-snacks
pacifiers. Soft skinned,
endless possibility,
sprinkled in baby powder.

Beautiful – new birth of ideas
wet with wonder, glistening
fresh from imagination
makes way down the thought
canal into the world.

Beautiful – all-natural,
cuddle-friendly chest hair.

Yes it is beautiful!
So, men, leave it there!

## Dear Picasso

Women do not have both eyes
on one side of their noses.

We do not leave the house in a hat
and high heels, with everything
else exposed.

Oh, dear Picasso!

You knew the rules and how to
break them.  Your offerings birthed
from your demands.

A bit of genius – you danced
the avenue ahead of your time.
So – we understand.

## Misfire

When I find myself surrounded by people who repeatedly
hit the bulls-eye, I pray their impeccable aim rubs off,
and their presence is like good second-hand-smoke. May
their wisdom hang in the air and enter my brain
through my lungs.

May the shame of Misfire and the heavy weight of longing
peel from my skin like a layer of dead cells. May I live
lively and in some new way.

When wishing loses its grip on my ribcage, I lean into
the ease of the climb. I welcome the path that is mine.

No more hoping for return calls. No more nursing
a day gig and waiting for acceptance to be the reason
for the next breath, still worth taking.

## Lost and Round

I walked briskly. Left my fleeting mark on the
soft sandy shoreline and found myself sandwiched
between steady cool breeze at my back-warm sun rays
showered my face in blissful contrast on a lovely afternoon.

A walk in the sand is good for strengthening the
lower calf. I thought to myself as I glanced down
and suddenly noticed my bare feet (with moist
sand clinging to them) was missing my toe ring.

I felt annoyed with myself. I always lose things
that I like – boyfriends, enjoyable jobs, boyfriends,
etc, etc. Did I mention boyfriends?

Something told me not to wear it today. That is
what I get for not listening to "Something."

I imagined my toe ring, feeling lost and abandoned
by me, peeking half out of the sand somewhere.
It had watched me walk away with its little toe ring
with eyes full of tears. It still awaited my return.

I aimlessly wandered into a small shop
on the boardwalk and looked through the brightly
patterned wide skirts and then I saw the handmade sign
on the counter, "Sterling silver toe rings, on sale,
two for the price of one."

Suddenly, I imagined my old toe ring
had planned its escape! Fed up with being stepped on,
it triumphantly dove into the sand and is glad
to hand me over to some new toe ring.

**Can You Believe?**

Yesterday
I was talking to...
What's-his-name?

He said
he needed a new...
What-cha-ma-call-it

That is about so big,
you know?

I promised to pick it up
before I came over.

So...I set out...
Found myself lost...
Riding all over...
Who-knows-where

Looking for this...a
Thing-a-ma-gigga.

Anyhey,
I found it!
Had it next to my car.

Drove off and forgot it.
Can you believe?

# II.

# Tinder Flames

## In Whispers

I detect in your veins
The heat I know in my own blood.
I hear its most subtle whimper and sigh.

Its call drowns out the bark and hiss
of an entire city. Its sweetness –
sharp-pungent as a field of lavender.

Distance – a dull scissor at the cord
of our connection. You feel my fingers
at play in the hair of your forearm. Your
cologne whispers as I enter an elevator alone.

You can see clearly. You know I am love.
Love – breathing in air. Love – drinking in water.

Love – humming softly on a floor pillow
with a green notebook leaving blue
marks on white paper.

## Twin Light

The windy musical notes of a street festival
swept you close, then closer.
My world jolted under the quick
curve of your smile.

Your lighthearted "Hello" floated over
the chatter of the crowd and was new
to my ear. Yet, your unspoken ways talked
in a strong voice and my soul heard
the tone and belted the harmony.

The spark within me spun and marveled
its reflection as joyously as a girl at her
mirror on prom night.

My core knew a shift had taken hold
Just as the eye of the stove knows
the strike of the match can and will...

Slowly, my palm found a new home
against yours. My cheek landed a warm
resting spot on the strong swell of your shoulder.

Gone – iced tea for one on a lazy Sunday
evening while I haunt a favorite patio chair.

No more – TV that plays in a room
like a best friend recounting the events
of the day. The street lamps, the city
and the planet Earth melted

and left me to the sparkle in your eyes.
You – the Glow-that-Calls.

## The Stone

Love slows reflexes to a crawl.
It affects hearing like a fine
filter where only words that feed
its growth seep through.

Romance sways judgment, allows you
to dream deep with eyes open, drive
under-the-influence legally; no DUI arrests!

Some men should be required to wear
warning labels, "Touch at your own risk,
Contents hot enough to liquify a stone!
Contact can melt reasoning and

induce love-sickness. Once infected,
two aspirin will do nothing. Do not call
any medical professionals in the morning,
They can not help you. Love symptoms will
be accompanied by high fever.... Accept it!"

## Soul Season

When you look at me like that,
I forget my name.

I forget my address,
I do not recall the appropriate
hour to go home.
What...did... I... wear... here?

You give me "that look"
and I am beside myself.
Am I to my left or to my right?

Am I getting ahead of myself?
Is it me that is behind?

I'm not feeling like myself.
Who do I feel like?

I see you
seeing me –

Everything else
a blur.

## Bona Fide Valentine

Funny how laughter and togetherness
fuel a sense of well-being and purpose.
Surprising how emotions can roar at
their depths while calm and subdued
at the surface.

My happiness soars. I sink, submerge
and fluff pillows on the couch next to you.
My mind, flooded with a complete loss
of words, met strong, delicate
understandings we grew.

You have built a home within the beat
of my heart, my tender bona fide Valentine.
Your love faces me down, protects me
at my side, shadows my steps from behind.

As warm as the center of a Sunday oven
in the winter. As certain as the returning
rush of the tide. Sweeter than the heart
shaped chocolates you bring me, your love
is bona fide!

# Damsel

What would I do without you?

Simple-mighty stir of wind shows fangs.
Snatches innocent-accomplice tree branch,
for feather-like deposit in the path of our
unsuspecting home-bound car.

Breaks prove themselves a gallant savior.
Now, your closeness intertwines
with a hue of safety around our movements.

Your closeness brushes away the tension
threatening to bite my belt buckle
and claw the collar and sleeves of my shawl
while angry mud grabs at every step
of my high heels.

It is your voice that calms me as we
quick-blink the toss of small particles
dealt by the hand of the gust.

"Everything is going be alright" you say
and the curve of the black road flashes a ray
of hope, a light winking in a distant window.
You-being-you-being-close helps me believe.

What would I do without you?

## Loitering in the Doorway

I want you.
I just don't care to marry.

Ridiculous statement
I made to my man.

I vow to

Be neither here nor there.
Be neither in, nor out.
Not with you, I'm just not gone.

I vow we

Can build on un-solid ground
of shallow commitment.

Please tolerate
my wasting your time.

Coddle my excuses and apprehension,
accept prolonged nothingness,
holding you in suspension.

He said – "Time to move forward,
no sitting on the stairway.
I love you. Why loiter in the doorway?"

"Step with me to where love is on-track."
Filled with fear, foolishly I stepped back.

# The Offering

## An Ode to the Ural Owl

The wisdom of Gods
in my heartbeat.
The breathe of earth
brush my wings.

My eyes carry the black of midnight
to dance in the light of day.
Then, graciously usher the black
back to its seat in darkness.

My swoop is like an ancient
language in tall letters on the winds.
My call can bully the forest floor
Be silence all within!

A gallant suitor offers his humble
fresh and furry catch.
We feast – then become
a twosome perched on a
warm, soft wooden nest.

# Paperweight

If I were a paperwight,
I would sit on juicy love
letters. I would guard
their romance like
a decorated General.

I would protect them from
spills from coffee, gusts of
breezes. I would hold in place
the glow of their importance.

If I could choose what I'm
made of – a material that's unbreakable.
I would not wish to loose
myself should the letters be snatched
and torn up after a lovers' quarrel.

Only that could cause me
to relinquish my duties.

## Prey

He entered the hall
All swagger and calm.

A "Him-ness" unhomogenized
by the opinion of "They."

A million lights touched
my spine, tingled my toes.

My eyes, devoid of blinking
studied his movement.

Welcome to the dance
of fighting fire with fire.

One female catches scent
of prey on the hunt.

## Quake

His expression is all
drum-tired-of-the-beat.

He is fanged-angel limp
with hunger, half past 31.

His story collides (120 mph)
With Miss 20-any-day-now,
fashionista.

Land-mine in high heels,
burgundy hat and raw
uncertainty on her sleeves.

She is safe as lettuce
in a salad bar. He is all
shark on her new blood.

Caution is just
so "last-season."

## Un-intimacy

Two ships sinking in the sight
of each other.

We float from closeness into
being strangers-with-history.

Deaf-hearted on turbulent waters
an emotional language scrambled
in its signal.

Love lost like driftwood
in the surf. You become a fog horn
on a shore,

A comfort only if you are
at a safe distance.

## Bat of the Eye

The happiness that once
lived in her eyes was
cased out – homeless

Finely dressed with a
personality like a bent
can that fell from
a recycling bend.

Hollow-with-a-twist.
What was once smooth
is now raged edges.

Her look damned the day,
prayed for time-travel to
transport her back to the
age of 27.

The day before she met-him.

## Still Life with Bird

A candle couple's rendezvous is
intruded by the flutter of wings.

The female candle looks across at
her lover with her face all aflame.

He is smokey-eyed as he gazes back at
her and says, "Honest, babe, I don't know
this bird. Never seen her before in my life."

Two thick wax droplets run slow down
the side of his face.

The knife looks up at the wine bottle and
whispers, "I am sure I have seen Mr. Candle

on another night at another table, smoldering
with this same bird on the scene, dancing
around, shaking her tail feather."

## Betrothal to Etch

Rice should be thrown,
bells should be rung.
Bare skin and etch
vow to take the plunge.

I solemnly promise
buzz of needle to bear.
I do, take the color
to carry and wear.

One willing human canvas
captures lifetime design
of intrigue and symbols –
rebellion combined.

On display, from this day,
a break from the obscure
wings stand on shoulder for
freedom won, or procured.

One expression with back-story
verbally seldom told.
The fantasy-lover's face
stares wide-eyed and bold.

## Desire

Claims a heart –
no break of skin.
Commands the pupil
of the eye – Widen!

Triggers denial.
Bends the mind to blame
the soles of shoes
when feet linger
long in one place.

Oh, this quickening beat
of the heart in a crowded café
is caused not by this
hunk-of-a-man.

It is the caffeine!
Just the caffeine and
an overwhelming need
for... more... coffee.

# Couple

Two people, cuddled in one blanket,
gaze at a blinking Christmas tree.
Breaths and hearts in unison.
Silence speaks loudly of contentment
She is yin to his yang.
He is apple of her desire.

Two people scolded by the heat
of an argument. Stubbornly rooted
in the center of their living room. Yell over
one another until numb in the eardrums.
Silence speaks loudly of resentment.
She is the thorn in his side.
He is the pain in her neck.

Two people swept up in the rapture
of renewed vows. Look knowingly,
tearfully into the familiar corners
of one another's soul.
His thumbs gently stroke her finger
as they hold hands. Silence speaks loudly
of alignment. She is the M in Muse
He is the B in Backbone.

Two people; side by side on a hill,
turned peacefully toward the sky.
Near stone proclamation of long fruitful life
silence speaks loudly of eternal entwinement.
She is the warmth in the afternoon breeze.
He – the moonbeam in the night sky.

# III.

# Elixir Cafe

## Mud in Magic

It is to spend time on a funky junction,
overlook the "how" and become
"I don't know." It is to wear an early-bird
coat with full feathers when the entire
event is late. It is to find that one has tricked
the trickster, turned the tables on the
bait-and-switcher...and got a free ticket.

It is to take life too serious. Put the squeeze
on what is not right-for-you, feel it sting
the palm of your hand like a bumble bee
on the blind side of an apple...but win the bushel.

Mud in magic can be welcome, as "loud"
at the library, "quiet" at an amusement park,
fun as a root canal one day before the feast.
It can murk up the view of a clear day then dry
quickly. It is the moment a way with words does
not win one a way with other things wanted.

It is to select a fall-from-grace, show that taste
buds are dull or absent from the mouth altogether.
It is to be drunk on foolishness, shame one's way
up the side of the nearest mountain, then watch
the seeds evolve into practical moves.

Proof in the face, some stumble and win the race
one foot behind the other; however triumphant
or tragic. The low-down on high-life appears
that dry desert has hidden moisture
and there are obvious bits of mud in magic.

## Alabama Hills

If stone could talk, If rock could call out,
what secrets would its dusty voice reveal?

Would it tell of the teardrops that fell on
the slopes or how weary the feet walking near?

Oh, Alabama Hills, unyielding and proud,
boast emotions of gray, brown and blue.

I've seen raindrops dance in joy
on your peaks, birds abandon their
flight just for you.

You stand rubbing elbows with heaven,
Offering the coolness found in your shade.

I've seen a boulder drop heavily down,
from the crease of a frown that you made.

## Up for Air

Cuddled at midnight, with my pillow of dread,
I and apprehension lay like spoons in my bed.
My suffocating "To Do" list, too long for one person.
Its tedious tasks make my aching head worsen.

My stubborn impatience has landed me here.
I want it all now. I want it last year.
I hold anger so big over things that are small,
like my neighbor's loud laughter while
bouncing a ball.

I can choose to narrow my focus singly on a plan,
long enough to get myself fully in hand.
Wrapped warm in my blankets, my emotions are bare
as I promise myself, to pull me up for air.

## Stitches

Day three in my corner
next to the door near
soft sofa-quiet progress.

I knit as family moves around me
Their day swollen with bustling
activity...

I stitch in one direction then the
other. Stop for late afternoon room
temperature snack-no extra salt,
few additives.

Then back to knitting - waiting
later listening to family discussions
haggling who's turn to clear the dishes.
Listen to young Tony struggle with homework.

Their laughter-sadness-secrets are like
particles in the air fall like dust on
my knitting.

Day four I am greeted by hand of
fate. Fickle-hand holds a spray bottle.
Its mist paralyzes, burns my eight eyes
brings poisonous end to my stitches.

## Until Now

Until now it was fine
to make the best of shallow water
and not challenge life above the knee.

As we hunger for afterglow,
we step as sure-footed as a walk
on thin ice can guarantee.

The naked, the raw, the boldly
ungraceful also reach for the new
and make the best of a willingness
to step bold then fall through.

Yes, small fish in a drying lake
can hear the belly-laugh of the sun.
Life on the edge – cut with dull
scissors – until now, was so fun.

## Compassion

**C** is for comfort; when you need rest.
        soak down and weary.

**O** is for Oodles; the hugs I give when
        eyes are teary

**M** is for Mindful: no sharp edged words
        will I select.

**P** is for Pardon; more forgiveneess
        than you expect.

**A** is for Acute; your suffering calls
        me to react.

**S** is for Seeing; myself within you
        looking back.

**S** is for Sensitive; your emotions show
        their bleeding wounds.

**I** is for Intuition; your tough appearance
        just a cocoon.

**O** is for Open; I truly hear
        when you express

**N** is for Nurture; collective dreams
        to manifest.

## Saturday

Rain or shine, its 24-hour
embrace is ever so brief.

52 songs a year it can sing –
a tune of welcome relief

Saturday is here – we jump into now,
step back from demand and sweat
on the brow.

No alarms to alarm us or time-clocks
to visit. Saturday is as life was intended.

Early stroll, late brunch, be it shared or
Alone.  Time-currency, we get to spend it.

Nature, being wise and kind, gave us
an extra pillow named Sunday.

Knowing it could be too much for the mind
if Saturday fell into Monday.

## Morning Moonrise

Stopped on the freeway, I notice the Moon
has clocked in for the morning shift.

What a hostile territory for the Moon.
The Sun glares jealously, upstaging it.
The Blue Sky joins in to downplay it.
Even the gridlock is a tad disrespectful
of its beauty.

The Moon hangs there, ignored
and brokenhearted as a jilted lover.
I long to tell the Moon to clock out at once
and report back to its post at 9:00 p.m.

How could the Moon forget the Night Sky
that faithfully and gladly compliments its glow
or the Stars, the willing chorus of
background singers for its flashy show?

## All in a Day

Morning, full of hope, peeked yellow eyelashes over
the hills and stretched her long fingers of light. This
jarred the Marine Layer to run and catch a bus.

As Marine Layer ran, he called over one shoulder
to Midday who marched in, blew his hot breath
on the landscape and stomped in circles
until losing its footing.

Then, Midday rolled clumsily into Afternoon,
waking her from her nap on the hammock. Afternoon
jumped up and went for a long run, she paused only
once to gaze at a group of Rabbits playing in a field.

Eventually, Afternoon jumped on her tired legs over
Evening who had crawled in on hands and knees
and tried to get a drink from a broken water fountain.

Later, Evening wrapped herself in a colorful jacket
And turned on her side with her back to Nighttime.
This caused Nighttime to feel sad, push in heavy
clouds.

Their tears tapped lightly at windows, as Nighttime
laid flat on his back and prayed for the hope of
Morning.

## Later

Finally it is summer!
July's Joy waxes into a need
to escape the heat in a no-escape
trek across a parking lot to a
flurry of summer sales.

The hot days melt into an even
hotter evenings. Now married to
July, we get burnt by it. Impulse
buys sprout into buyers' remorse.

Later... we eye October longingly
on the calendar. Its arms – inviting.
Its cool – irresistible! We can hardly wait!

October arrives to bring us watery
eyes, sneeze after sneeze. Up its sleeves
are dry leaves to burn the nose.

Later... it will be great when December
gets here, with its cheer, twinkling lights,
familiar songs and colors.

December rolls through with an endless list
of tasks, to bruise the shoulders under stress.

Later ... we look ahead to March when
the cost of December will be done with.
We will be past Valentine's day pressure –
the arguments about it... put-to-sleep by March.

March kicks in the door. Its ticks like a
time bomb. How many week's until
the property tax deadline?...Oh the stress!

We look forward to (later) the relief of
up-coming vacation plans warm-long
days, getaways Just can't wait until...July.

**Next**

From the tip-top of January
to the bottom of every December,
life is a continuum.
May we remember to remember.

There are no platforms on which we
halt. No arrivals at which we are landing.
There is only continuous movement.
Blend motion into all planning.

Next is a good four letter word that dances
on the tongue and illuminates the playgrounds
of our minds. Next can call loudly or soft
and subtle when it chimes.

Within the cold of winter remember next are
the fragrant flowers of spring. Next reminds us
there is no be-all or end-all to anything.

When riding a high tide or if a low tide
has you feeling sadness or perplexed,
know true muscle can be found
 in how well we just say... Next!

## Made in...

The sun dances a can-can through the near by window on a crisp morning. I am keeping a hot cup of tea company when my gaze falls on the proud "Made in England" proclamation printed on the slumbering tea sleeve lying lazy on the table.

Imagine each of us embossed with "Made in" notifications that not only announced our country, but the exact location of our creation placed delicately by the almighty in our native language.

Just imagine "Made in 57 Chevy-Santa Monica Pier" across the top of someone's back.... or "Made in Honolulu, Hawaii" (on honeymoon), printed on another.

In the future, some adults could have a notice, "Made in a California laboratory dish."
Just a thought.

## Traveler

I mill among the swipe of random
elbows; the push of a shoulder here,
the bump of a hip there.

I plant my bum in the cool of a sideways
seat, feel the train accelerate
along with a sea of "back stories"
known as other passengers.

Their expressions, like projectors in a
movie house. Some giggle in hush tones
toss words that do not reach my ears.
Non-blinking stares at assorted hand
gadgets or out the windows where their
vision chases the speeding lights that
glance in from the tunnels.

Still, others show the weight of the day
in down-cased eyes and the slump
of shoulders. I reach my stop and sail
quickly through sliding doors,
into the glide of the nearest "up"
escalator. Three steps ahead,

a baby gazes at me, as his little cheek rubs
the safety of his mother's shoulder. He
smiles widely and then laughs as if
he can see the cartoons that I watched
a few hours earlier, all it's slap-stick
in replay on my forehead or as if a gang
of Looney tunes hitched a ride, like
a hat upon my hat.

## Walls Fell Down – Arrival in India

As I stepped out of the airport at 1:08 am,
the monsoon heat greeted me with a full
body press. Its breath fogged my eyeglasses
like a sauna.

A large crowd of taxi men vied for the attention
of our group. They waved and shouted as they
pushed each other. I rolled my shoulders
in readiness like a swimmer at the first sign
of "how-deep-the-waters." I searched through
this sea-of-men and found a driver
with my name held high across his chest.

The next day, as the car wheels tackled the long
ride from Mumbai to Pune, walls within me fell
down and were washed away by the countless
waterfalls flowing down the sides of the mountains.

Walls fell down with the fleeting sight
of a family of monkeys that trotted free
along the side of the road. Walls fell down
amidst the glow of common-ground –
conversations shared in the car.

The old me died a death so sudden
that I paused to pay my former self
a respectful moment of silence.

# The Mist

It's 8:30 pm. I become aware of the cold
temperature of the station bench through
my clothing. The train's headlight appears
on the track, a distant sun blinking so far off
there is no warmth from its rays.

The feeling draws me back to our afternoon
meeting announcement that a re-organization
is about to disorganize my life and reveal
accumulated dust in its corners.

It's funny how one sentence can tighten temples,
add pepper and vinegar to a fresh cup of coffee
and suck all the air from the room at the same time.

These moments come out of the mist,
bringing a chilly foul odor with a perfume
label. An appointment with insomnia placed
before me with the dash of a stiff smile.

Back at my desk, my attention creeps over
to the upside. I recall insomnia visiting me
with increased frequency over the past two years.

Let me see: demands, aching hands and insomnia
versus insomnia and a new start. The cup
before me was suddenly half full. It is not
too sweet, but it has some cream.

## Spiral

Notions caught in the wind.
Spun into a bonfire like
seeds wasted on infertile ground.

Children walk a path true
to the dance of growth and change.
An agreement unspoken, given
and kept with mother nature
and her father...Time.

Their proud gaze is unpredictable,
unmeasured and musical.

Parents preach to accumulation
generation that less is more. Their words
are more or less bounced away by deaf ears.

The message stepped on
like last week's cigarette;
dropped underfoot with other
former flames forgotten,

rudely trampled at the starting line
like many fancy, silly early notions.

## A Tune

Messages blare
from the core of the soul

Ring so loud and clear

Tit-bits and secrets
glisten like gold

heard only by internal ear.

This tune throbs, its rhythm
drives me into dancing

in sync with the beat
of my pulse.

Ideas, truths and blessed mistakes
swirl in a singular waltz.

## Smitten

Silence has a crystal ring
prettier than a Sunday bell.
I am smitten with Now.
A tiny sprout on an endless
tree of moments.

Hear 4:20 a.m. have very little to say.
Offers stirred stillness
with a side of hot tea.

Through a buffed window,
that invites the outpouring of light,
thoughts flow liquid-clear.

Before the swell of bird-call
Autumn sky fills
with a dry wind that naps
like an infant, warm and fed.

Yesterday's beastly unraveling
of disappointed expectancy is
swept away by the possibility broom.

It tumbles tail-first into a mental
trash receptor, rightfully forgotten,
like so many other yesterdays past.

## God Is

The voice under silence
loud with reason.
Purple buds and brown leaves
that color seasons.

God is motor that powers
our every breath.
God is drum for heartbeats
within every chest.

In the burst on the surface
of billions of suns,
in the scorch of volcanoes,
God heats every one.

God resides in bubbly laughter
of babies, in wind-giving-flight.
In the solid ground, that breaks a fall.

In the cold that caps mountains
with snow. Both near and far.
God is All within
All.

## Home Sweet Home

Dipped in crisp-dry boredom. Then the sweat
of surprise. Always, home sweet home
I peek out through brown eyes.

I welcome each bum without pulling away.
Content, like the sculptor,
hands push life as clay.

Around the slant of a road, through the slip
of a valley, up the dark of staircases,
down the stink of the alleys.

Bruised by loose rock from the path
I am on. Yet I ease into safety,
wrapped in resolve and calm.

## Chapter Done

How many more labored breaths
will we witness?
Life on the runway back into light.

Memories of laughter gleam,
golden in weight and measurement.
Tugs-of-war hold as pointless
powder-under-foot.

Another moment falls into dust
Like tiny invisible pillars sawed
away by the mere tick of seconds.

Embarkation and sorrow cave into one.
Edge of closure and a new beginning.
This chapter – done!

## The Back Word

Another page turned on the journey of a happy loner who loves storytelling, art and music as much as Kokopelli loves seeds and a flute.

When I look back at my past life events that inspire some of my writing, it is only to retrieve a new lesson by viewing the circumstances from a new angle. Thoughts that make being-in-the-now, even richer. I am serious about keeping-life-light-and-fun.

I fall, I get back up, I fall, I get back up...It gives me a lot of practice at getting back up. I am very proud to say, I have a doctorate at laughing at myself. So there!

If your eyes have made it to this page, I hope you have enjoyed this book and detect a different message on the same pages next time you read it. I am wishing you a tremendous life filled with new adventures, joy and that you give yourself permission to just be you.

**The End**

# About the Poet

Beverly M. Collins is fourth in a family of five daughters. Although born in Milford, Delaware, Bev is a Jersey-girl to the bone. She is also a graduate of Taylor Business Institute, a great admirer of Art who carries a deep appreciation and respect for other Artists.

As a singer, Collins is a former national finalist for Talent America. As a poet, she is one of three 2012 prize winners for the California State Poetry Society whose works appear in a growing number of publications.

At home with her younger family members, she is Auntie Bev. The one who loves to cook, laugh and watch movies, enjoys amusement parks and the peacefulness of a long walk. She loves the sound of great guitar solos and times spent in complete silence where thoughts reign ...Many of which have floated to the pages of this book; her second collection of poetry. May you enjoy and relate.

Photo by C. T. Mallier

www.ingramcontent.com/pod-product-compliance
Lightning Source LLC
Chambersburg PA
CBHW031205090426
42736CB00009B/787